This book belongs to:

_____

Om Baby
Child of the Universe

written and illustrated by
Schamet Horsfield

An Om Baby Book
www.ombabyworld.com

Grateful
acknowledgment
to my family,
friends, and community.

Thank You!

Special Thanks to:
Nina Barnett, Zan Tewksbury, Bob and Eden Sky,
Heather and Brian Main, Gray Horsfield, and Jeremy Bennett.

Published in 2010 by Om Baby World , LLC
Seattle, Washington
www.ombabyworld.com

Text set in Polo-SemiScript Ex

10 9 8 7 6 5 4 3 2 1

Manufactured in Singapore by Imago
First Edition, March 2010

ISBN-13: 978-0-9825200-1-7
ISBN-10: 0982520018
Library of Congress Control Number: 2009912595

The contents of this book are printed with soy based inks on paper
from responsibly managed forests and contain 25% post-consumer recycled fiber.

Hi, My name is Om Baby.
I am an Om Being from a small community called Omville.
I have only one eye because
I see the world and all beings as one.
Om Beings (hum-om-beings) believe in love, peace, and unity.
Om is the Sanskrit word and symbol that means "all that is."
I wear the Om symbol close to my heart so that I always remember...
I am a child of the universe.

Om Baby
loves
his mother.

Om Baby
loves
his father.

Om Baby
believes in
family, friends,
and unity.

Om Baby
is
peaceful.

Om Baby
is
kind.

Om Baby believes in the power of his mind.

Om Baby
loves
adventure.

Om Baby
loves
to read.

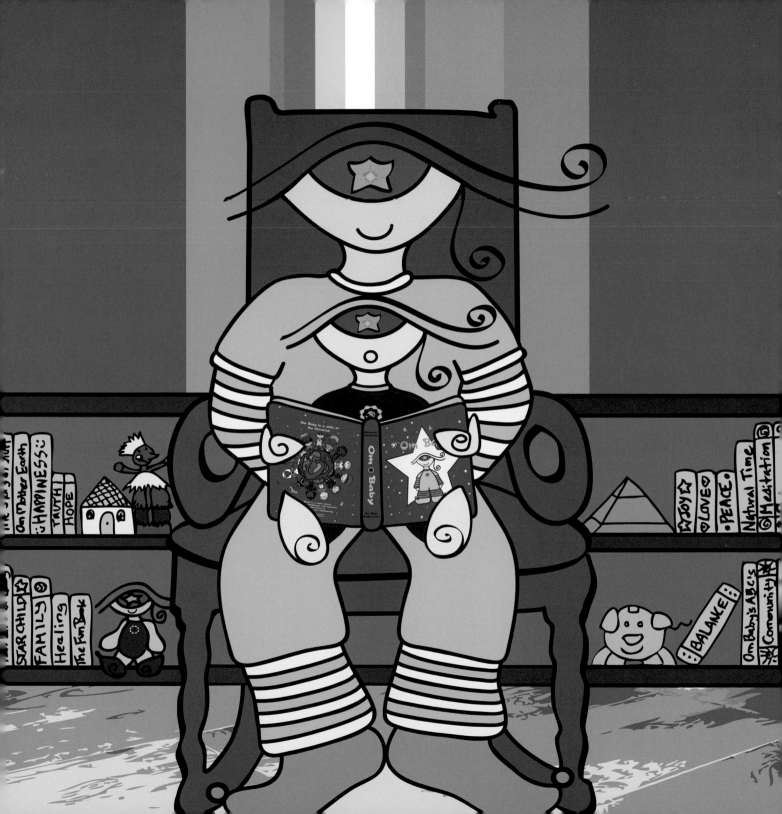

Om Baby
loves science,
art, and mystery.

Om Baby
does
yoga.

Om Baby
eats
his greens.

Om Baby
loves to dance
and sing.

Om Baby
believes in
truth, love, and
community.

Om Baby
recycles.

Om Baby
plants
trees.

Om Baby
believes in his
dreams.

Om Baby
loves rocketships
to the moon.

5,4,3,2,1

Blast off Om Baby!

Om Baby was inspired by the birth
of my son Octavius.
I wanted to create a character
who would teach him about our
responsibility to the earth and to each other.
Om Baby represents
the most important things in life:
love, truth, and unity.

Om Baby is the light and love within us all.
Have you hugged your inner Om Baby today?

Photograph by: Sergio Ortiz © sergiophotography.net

For more information please visit us at:
www.ombabyworld.com

Om Baby really does plant trees!
For each Om Baby book made, a tree is planted.
For more information please visit:
www.ecolibris.net